La

A true and sweet friend!

Blessings!

June

I have known the Whatleys for over twenty years. I was privileged to be their pastor for most of that time before they moved to Tennessee. In *#Life Change,* June takes a wide-angled lens approach to the journey of following Jesus as Savior and Lord. She details crucial points of reference on this journey. Every chapter brings a focus on the "Light". A strong prophetic element has characterized June's experiences and ministry. When she speaks of pain, it is because she has been through multiple crucibles of life. I really believe *#Life Change* will greatly impact a searching heart, a hungry heart, a desperate heart. June wrote, "The truth is, if we never got hurt, we would be living in a world without free will." So exercise your free will to open your mind and heart to the message of this book. The message will bring healing to your hurts.

Charles D. Lenn, Senior Pastor,
First Assembly of God, Tuscaloosa, Alabama

#LifeChange

A Treasure Hunt for More!

June Breland Whatley,
MA Counseling/Edu

WESTBOW
PRESS®
A DIVISION OF THOMAS NELSON
& ZONDERVAN

THE HOLY BIBLE, NEW INTERNATIONAL VERSION®,
NIV® Copyright © 1973, 1978, 1984, 2011 by Biblica, Inc.®
Used by permission. All rights reserved worldwide.

Scriptures marked KJV are taken from the KING JAMES
VERSION (KJV): KING JAMES VERSION, public domain.

WestBow Press books may be ordered through
booksellers or by contacting:

WestBow Press
A Division of Thomas Nelson & Zondervan
1663 Liberty Drive
Bloomington, IN 47403
www.westbowpress.com
1 (866) 928-1240

ISBN: 978-1-5127-5091-1 (sc)
ISBN: 978-1-5127-5092-8 (hc)
ISBN: 978-1-5127-5090-4 (e)

Library of Congress Control Number: 2016912010

Print information available on the last page.

WestBow Press rev. date: 08/10/2016

Contents

Introduction

Do you wish you could get more out of life? More joy? Better prospects? Are you happy, but you believe that there needs to be more to life? Are you at a place in life where you feel that you need a change? Are all areas working well, except one? Is there no area in your life working well? Or do a few areas seem to be working, but you still feel that something is missing?

Do you have regrets, loss, grief, sadness, loneliness, or emptiness? Are you in a state of deprivation or fear? Have you been abandoned emotionally or physically? Have you been abused, used or lied to? Are you *Angry*? Do you continue to make the same mistakes over and over again?

Most people can answer "yes" to at least one of these. Some people can answer "yes" to several.

In order to meet your needs, have you tried the usual comforts: food (whether chocolate, chips or pizza); the newest self-help book; the newest fad, craze, or religion; partying, drugs or alcohol; a new mate; a new job; a new place—but you still feel miserable? Well, maybe not miserable, but you do not feel full. No matter what you have tried, is there still something lacking?

Would you like to be able to change your outlook on life? Do you wish you could go on social media and type in *#LifeChange* and instantly fix everything?

Well, it may not be as instantaneous as you would like, but you can get there. It's a bit like a very important treasure hunt. So....

On to the Treasure Hunt!

Start here and now. Commit to trying *#LifeChange*. Work on it—while it works in you.

Treasure Hunt Clue Number 1, you must realize that you are in a war.

Say what???

Read on....

Treasure Hunt Clue Number 1

#You_Are_in_a _War

Recently, I had a very disturbing dream. It was set in a dark, dystopian world. The place was dirty, drab and seemed devoid of hope. People scrambled to survive.

From my vantage point, it appeared that the few refugees whom I could see lived in a dim, dingy compound of sorts. The buildings were in shambles; the windows and doors—draped with rags. It was stark. No hint of color. No hint of joy. The scene spoke of existence, but not of life. It was like a "land of the shadow of death."[1]

---

[1] Mt 4:16 NIV, "The people living in darkness have seen a great light; on those living in the land of the shadow of death a light has dawned."
Lk 1:79a NIV, "to shine on those living in darkness and in the shadow of death,"

The clothing of the cowering survivors was dull, dirty and tattered. Their faces and hair marred by the filth of their struggle. But before I could take it all in, the darkness of their world was split by a gigantic beam of Light. It was like a huge search beam, but from where? No one knew, and no one knew why it had come.[2]

They had seen others of their number who were touched by the Light and how drastically they had been changed. The changed ones seemed alien, sometimes crazed with hardly a hint left of their old selves.[3] They fled the safety of the compound for who knows what reason.[4] Their radical change[5] terrified the untouched ones.

---

[2] Jn 8:12 NIV, "'I am the light of the world. Whoever follows me will never walk in darkness,'"

Jn 12:46 NIV, "I have come into the world as a light, so that no one who believes in me should stay in darkness."

Acts 26:18a NIV, "to open their eyes and turn them from darkness to light,"

[3] 2 Cor 5:17 NIV, "the new creation has come: The old has gone, the new is here!"

1 Jn 2:8 NIV, "because the darkness is passing and the true light is already shining."

[4] 2 Cor 6:14 KJV, "and what communion hath light with darkness?"

2 Cor 5:17 NIV, "the new creation has come: The old has gone, the new is here!"

[5] 1 Jn 2:8 NIV, "because the darkness is passing and the true light is already shining."

Eph 5:8 NIV, "For you were once in darkness, but now you are light.... Live as children of the light."

Each time the Light approached, the fugitives hurriedly scooped up their meager treasures and tried to hide them. Among these possessions, a strand of pearls or other precious jewels could occasionally be glimpsed. They would quickly wrap them in their rags to secure them from the Light. Then, an instant before the Light arrived, they buried their faces in the filthy rags. Soon the prying Light would pass over and be gone.[6]

As the Light faded into the distance, the terrified vagabonds slowly emerged from their hiding places and peered into the dimly lit courtyard. The first time, as I cautiously crept from my hiding place, I noticed that the compound was enclosed by a wall or fence built of gray, weathered wood. With my eyes gradually adjusting to the dimness, I could see symbols on the fence. Advancing closer, I could see that they were large hashtags (#). They appeared to be splashed randomly on the stockade-like structure.

Very curious! What could they mean?

Again and again, day after day, the Light scanned and searched as the refugees dove for the

---

2 Cor 4:6 NIV, "Let the light shine out of darkness."
[6] Jn 12:35 NIV, "You are going to have the light just a little while longer. Walk while you have the light, before darkness overtakes you."

cover of a dark corner and hid in terror. After each passing of the Light, when I emerged from hiding, my attention was diverted to the fence, but the desperate rag-tag band stumbled around in fear as they had done on all of the previous occasions after the Light had vanished. They seemed oblivious to the growing number of hashtags which were displayed openly for all to see.

By now, several large symbols appeared like graffiti displayed along the fence. It was then that this thought was planted in my mind: "# is the name of the Light!"

Suddenly, as dreams are prone to do, I was transported to another place and into a different scene. I found myself outside in a lovely, open, grassy field. I was greeted by a gentle breeze and a clear, blue sky overhead. As I began to walk forward, I noticed that I was being joined by others. I did not know who they were or where they came from; nor did I know where we were going, but our numbers slowly increased, as we strode forward.

Starting up the gentle slope of the hill, a shack or building began to come into view on the horizon. As we neared the structure, I could now see that it appeared to be the shambles of an old house. In anticipation, I surged closer. No, not a house; oddly, it looked more like a wooden boat partially, submerged beneath earth and grass, but a possible safe haven nonetheless.

Just as we neared our destination, a yell rang out that sent people scurrying. Trying to figure out what to do, I paused and saw what appeared to be pirate avatars chasing the fear-filled pilgrims. I ran forward, looking for shelter, but found none. Without warning, my way was blocked by an evil, cartoonish-looking creature springing toward me. I awoke suddenly.

For days following the dream, I pondered the various pieces and symbols in the dream, I came to realize that the Light which searched the dim, dingy places in the first scene was trying to rescue the people, but they did not understand and feared the Light.

They did not want to relinquish their hold on the rags and trinkets that they treasured. They took everything they had that was clean and white and hid it from the Light. The pearls and jewels were concealed, without knowing that those gems could have been enriched and used greatly when touched by the Light. Instead, hidden within the rags of their world, their treasures were worthless and wasted. Fearing the change that they had seen in others, they refused to surrender to the Light. They did not know that the Light could end their lonely, hopeless struggle.

The sojourners in the next scene represented people who had been liberated by the Light, but who still searched for what they thought would be a safe place to live or at least to rest. As often happens in life, their quest was interrupted by evil avatars attacking the untrained warriors. They resorted to their past pattern of running to hide because they didn't know how to fight. They did not understand the power of the Light.

Many who will read this book have already experienced the Light, but may lack the skills they need for warfare. These people should make no mistake about it—we're all in a war![7] This book, *#LifeChange* is not only an attempt to teach those who are in the Light how to overcome the darkness and how to fight, but also to introduce the Light to those who are willing to come out of the darkness.

---

[7] Eph 6:12 NIV, "For our struggle is not against flesh and blood, but against the rulers, against the authorities, against the powers of this dark world and against the spiritual forces of evil in the heavenly realms."

Let's look at some of the struggles in life that keep people down and how people can persevere and be victorious.

#Regret

There is a song by *Big Daddy Weave* that I really like. It starts like this:

> Seems like all I can see was the struggle
> Haunted by ghosts that lived in my past
> Bound up in shackles of all my failures[8]

Are you haunted by ghosts of regret from your past? Are you bound in chains of your past failures? A song by Josh Wilson puts it this way:

> Oh, I know it all too well
> Every inch inside this cell
> I'm a prisoner of the choices I regret[9]

---

[8] Big Daddy Weave. "Redeemed." By Mike Weaver and Benji Cowart. *Love Come To Life.* fervent Records. CURB Records. 2012. CD.

[9] Wilson, Josh. "No More." By Josh Wilson, Benji Cowart and Jeff Pardo. *That Was Then, This Is Now.* Sparrow Records. 2015. CD.

Do you feel like a prisoner? Are you held—bound—locked up by regret? Are your regrets the result of your own actions? Or were your regrets caused by someone else? Regardless, you can be set free. There is a way to freedom. It is the Light.

Most of us know the feeling of regret, but what is it? Where does it come from? What causes it? According to the *New Oxford American Dictionary,* regret can be to "feel sad, repentant, or disappointed over (something that has happened or been done, especially, a loss or missed opportunity)."

Are some of your regrets the result of something that has happened or something that has been done to you? Have you been hurt? It is virtually impossible to maneuver through life's maze without being hurt, but sometimes hurts are profound. Immoveable! Unforgettable! Unforgivable!(?)

Let's look at that last one first. The strange thing about unforgiveness is that it ensnares you. It keeps you bound to the one who hurt you. Unforgiveness is a corrupt avatar who traps you in its snare.

Some people may say that they will *never* forgive a person because he or she hurt them too badly. Well, did you know that that person may not even remember the offense? But you have trapped yourself and bound yourself to that person and to that offense. Forgiveness doesn't change or erase the past, but it gives you the beginning of a different future.

It may be true that the person hurt you tremendously, but unforgiveness has you locked into a cycle of remembering and reliving the event. Take for instance the case of a rape. That is one of the most horrible, personal, torturous events I can imagine! You constantly live in its pain. You remember. You relive. You are constantly fearful. It never leaves. It never fades. You hate the one who hurt you.

You deserve justice! You deserve freedom! You deserve your life back again, but how? You can't undo the event. (It's immoveable.) You can't forget the horror. You can't remove the fear. You can't defeat the feeling of violation. (It's unforgettable.) But there is a remedy. It is the Light!

Some blame the Light for not protecting them. The truth is, if we never got hurt, we would be living in a world without free will. We would be puppets. That is not true here. In this world, the imaginations of a man's (or a woman's) heart are evil from an early age,[10] unless changed by the Light. In this life, we all get hurt, some worse than others, but the Light is not the cause. The Light wants to heal those hurts.

Here is how to start your healing:

- Ask the Light to break the cycle of torment. (Do you need a clue to the identity of the Light? Did you already know, or have you been checking the footnotes? If you don't know, I'll tell you the identity of the Light in a few pages, at the end of the section, #Grief.)

- Ask the Light to help you forgive the one who hurt you and to set you free. What? Forgive a rapist? **This DOES NOT mean that you think your attacker was right or justified. It DOES mean that your life will no longer be bound in pain and terror. As you begin to forgive, here's what happens—the one who hurt you will then begin to lose control over you! It is terribly difficult, but it is not impossible, with the help of the Light.**

---

[10] Gn 8:21 KJV, "for the imagination of man's heart is evil from his youth"

Did you know that as you forgive others, you open yourself up to being restored?[11]

- While forgiving the person who hurt you, you are actually beginning to regain control of your life. No longer hating that person, frees up the parts of your soul that unforgiveness had consumed.
- You cannot take hold of a new life while you are holding on to the old life. Unforgiveness is the rope that has had you tied. Let the Light untie the knots. I know this is hard, but what else can you do? Let the Light heal you.

This approach can work no matter what the offense, no matter how you were hurt—you can be free. Were you abandoned or neglected? Were you betrayed? Do you feel rejected? Are you bitter? Are you too needy? Are you constantly disappointed? Are your feelings damaged? Are you, as a result, ruining your relationships? Do you want to feel different? You can be free!

Turn loose of the rope of unforgiveness that has had you bound. It has not bound the one who hurt

---

[11] Mt 6:12 KJV, "Forgive us our debts as we forgive our debtors."

you; it has bound you. Feel the sense of relief as you give the rope to the Light for justice. Ask the Light to shine into your mind, your will and your emotions, and to set you free from unforgiveness. You can't change anything in the past, but you can laugh in the face of the avatar tormentor Unforgiveness, as you sense his grasp slipping away. You can begin to be free to rebuild your life with the aid of the Light.

Another area of regret that plagues people is regret of something they have done. This regret is also under the heading of remorse, which is a "deep regret or guilt for a wrong committed," as defined by the *New Oxford American Dictionary*.

Do you have regret or feel guilty because of something that you have done? Have you hurt someone? Abandoned someone? Tarnished someone's reputation? Have you committed a social blunder that embarrassed someone? Have you failed at a venture? Are you bound up in shackles of all your failures, as described by Big Daddy Weave in the song "Redeemed"?

Is what you've done irrevocable? Sometimes it is irrevocable, sometimes not. Sometimes an apology, a confession or a *Mulligan* will set things straight, but many times your regret remains. Do what you can to set things right, but sometimes you just need to learn to forgive yourself. That can be difficult, but did you know that refusing to forgive yourself is in essence saying that your judgment is higher or more righteous than the judgment of the Light?

The Light forgives your wrongs if you ask, and the Light will cleanse you from all the wrongs you have committed.[12]

So whether what you regret is revocable or not, changeable or not, re-doable or not; here is the answer: *Forget those things which are behind! Forgive yourself and move forward in life!*[13]

'Not easy,' you say. True, but the man who penned that sentiment was guilty of helping to track down early Christians and reporting them to Jewish authorities, in order that they could be imprisoned or even put to death. You can read about it in Acts 7:54-8:3.

---

[12] 1 Jn 1:9 KJV, "If we confess our sins, he is faithful and just to forgive us our sins, and to cleanse us from all unrighteousness."
[13] Phil 3:13 KJV, "this one thing I do, forgetting those things which are behind, and reaching forth unto those things which are before"

Was what he did irrevocable? Definitely! But he was able to move forward with the help of the Light. You can too! But you can't hold onto the past and move forward. That's impossible! The past will impede your progress. It will weigh you down, unless you turn to the Light to lighten your load.

#Loss

Does regret or remorse have you enslaved because of a loss you have suffered? Is your remorse in the area of a personal relationship that you have lost? Have you been left by a spouse, or a girlfriend or a boyfriend? I don't want to trivialize this. It is painful! People sometimes feel worthless, like they have nothing left to live for, but that is not true. It hurts, yes! But it is not fatal unless you make it so. Contemplating suicide is not a valid option. Suicide is another wicked avatar who can whisper into a person's ear. You must believe that your death would be deeply felt. 'Not true,' you say. You are wrong! The Light has a plan for you. The Light wants you healed and walking in His glow.

You *can* move on from feeling worthless to feeling valuable.

But how do you get over this kind of lost relationship?

1. First, you must realize that your value was never in that other person. Your value is within yourself, but it needs to be submitted to the brightness of the Light to bring out its true clarity and beauty.

2. Recognize that people have a right to withdraw from relationships. Whether right or wrong, it is their choice. They may withdraw because they are broken and hurting. Chasing them or stalking them never solves the problem.

3. You may desire to draw the person back into the relationship because it makes you feel more whole to have them around. But here is the truth, that person cannot fill your void. At best, he or she can only put a temporary patch on your pain. When the patch is ripped off, like an adhesive bandage, it hurts. There is no such thing as an ouch-less bandage for the heart.

4. I recognize that you may feel lonely, hurt and abandoned. Pause a moment to consider that one of the evil avatars from my dream can be named, Abandonment. If you have been abandoned it can leave a deep reservoir of hurt and emptiness. You must choose to let the Light wash away the emptiness and heal the pain.

5. But I must caution, if you are seriously depressed you may need to see a medical doctor. You may have a chemical imbalance or other issue that needs to be treated. Also remember that suicide is never the answer.

Another area of abandonment, whether you were physically or emotionally orphaned, is an absentee parent or parents. It can leave an empty space or large hole in a child's heart that lasts throughout adulthood. Some who were adopted as children, may think or feel that they must have been to blame. This is so unfair and not true.

I've heard it said that, 'broken people, break people.' Some broken people try to fill their ache with drugs or alcohol. Others try to fill their emptiness with another person. Either of these or both usually leave the child alone and uncared for or worse, abandoned.

Sometimes broken people know their limitations and they choose to give their child up for adoption in hopes that the child will have a better life. Even if your parent kept you, if your parent was hurting and broken, it is highly unlikely that he or she could have raised a whole and unhurt child. Adoption may have been a much better option for you. But if you are hurting and feel abandoned by your parent(s), ask the Light to heal you. The Light is willing and able to adopt and care for those who have been abandoned.[14]

If you choose not to call upon the Light, living without being healed can complicate things even further. Let's say that, as an adult, the person you are in a relationship with also abandons you; the hole inside you rips larger and deeper. What then?

- Over time and many repetitions, this can leave a chasm of immense proportion and cause deep emotional needs. The avatar of Deep Emotional Need is a cruel adversary.

---

[14] Ps 27:10 KJV, "When my father and my mother forsake me, then the Lord will take me up."

- The sinister avatars of Abandonment and Deep Emotional Need tell you that you are unworthy, or worthless, and no one can or will love you. Not true! The Light loves you!
- The most important thing that you must realize is that your chasm, your empty space, needs to be healed, not just filled. You might also need to see a physician, as well as to ask the Light to heal the chasm.[15] The Light sometimes works through doctors and medication. If you feel hesitant to see a doctor, keep in mind that if you were diabetic, you probably wouldn't hesitate to see a physician. Why should you not seek help for this if you need it?

Other Types of Loss

Maybe the loss you have suffered was the loss of a job, position or status. Have you suffered a loss that plagues you? This type of loss can play into a feeling of failure or unworthiness. Some may tell you, "There may be a better job, (position,

---

[15] Ps 147:3 NIV, "He heals the brokenhearted and binds up their wounds."

or status) in your future." "Perhaps you had to lose this job to free you for a future rise in placement." "Maybe that job wasn't what you thought it was."

These may be true, but may be too simplistic. Ask yourself some challenging questions.

- Perhaps you weren't prepared to excel in that place. Do you need more education?
- Was the loss caused by evil conniving? Behind-the-back conniving has displaced many a good worker, but were you lured into playing a part in it? Do you need counseling to make you wiser?
- Was your personality too abrasive or too weak for the task? Do you need coaching in management skills?

This may be an opportunity for you to:

- Get better prepared.
- Get a skill that makes you unique and/or find an empty niche that you can fill.
- Get counseling.
- Submit your talents and gifts to the Light.
- The Light can place you where you can flourish.

- Get healed and get prepared! There is a future ahead of you.

There are many possible scenarios. Too many to fully cover here, but try to apply these concepts to your particular situation.

#Grief

The *New Oxford American Dictionary,* defines grief as "deep sorrow, especially that caused by someone's death."

Is the loss you feel, the death of a person? Are you overcome by sorrow? Who is the sorrow for? Is it for the person who is gone? Or is it for yourself? Often we hold on to grief because we feel sorry for ourselves.

I'm not talking about a recent loss or death of a loved one. This grief is natural, even healthy; but grief can plague a person long after a proper mourning period has passed. At times, an avatar of Grief can attach to you. Sometimes a person gets caught in a web of grief and can't get out. Are you holding on to grief—or is it holding on to you?

Has death taken a spouse, parent, sibling, child, or other? One of the avatars that can stalk us is Grief caused by death. Often people believe that the Light is to blame, because He didn't intervene and prevent the tragedy. But Death is the cruel and merciless tormentor who took your loved one; don't blame it on the Light. The 'what ifs' and 'whys' are never solved by blaming the Light. Realize that the Light is available, even searching, beckoning you to come and be consoled and healed. Don't make your rescuer the scapegoat for your pain.

Sometimes people may be afraid to let go of grief because they think it might imply that they didn't love the deceased person. Or they may be afraid that if they let go of grief that people will forget their loved one? Well neither of those is true. You can remember a person long after he or she is gone. You can love a person and still let them go.

Ask yourself some hard questions. Is that person in a better place? (Do you believe there is a better place?) Is he or she free from pain? Would he or she want to come back?

One question you should try not to ask is, "Why?" You may never get a satisfying answer, but to be healthier, you must let go of the grief.

Remember, that does not mean that you must turn loose of the memories of the person.

Sometimes another evil avatar at work is Guilt. Do you feel responsible for the person's death? Short of murder, there is little you can do to take a life. Sometimes accidents happen due to carelessness. Sometimes accidents happen due to a lack of expertise or foresight. These situations can lead to a deep place of guilt. You can run the scenario in your head a million times, but it doesn't change the circumstance. What happened cannot be changed. It happened. You need to give yourself some grace! Accidents *can* happen! But you must let go of the guilt and make it let go of you! Ask the Light to help you to break Guilt's hold on you and to be able to forgive yourself.

An exception is, did you intend for the person to die? That is different. Perhaps you feel that you need to be punished. If so, take it to the proper authorities. It is better to be confined in a jail cell than to be confined in your own mind by guilt. You need to ask the Light to help you. You can be forgiven.

This is not the boat that most people are in who suffer with grief or guilt. You may not be holding on to the grief or guilt, they may be holding on to you. There are those menacing evil avatars from the dream that can hold on to us in our life. You become an unwilling participant in a sinister game that you are allowing to be played.

What do I mean that 'you are allowing (it) to be played'?

- Recognize that grief or guilt is the devil's game and that you are being drawn in.
- Ask the Light to help you to stop facilitating the game and to stop cooperating!
- Ask Him how to break free.
- Ask Him to break the bonds that hold you.
- Sometimes the Light needs to show you what bonds have been forged and how to get out of them. Then you can, take action!

What action?

- Call off the game. When those thoughts of grief or guilt attempt to take your mind captive, tell them that you now know their scheme and that you refuse to play. Even if you have to repeat this step over and over in the beginning, with the help of the Light, you can break the hold that the wicked avatars of Grief, Guilt, Sorrow or Regret have on you.[16]

- Press on, look forward, retake control of your life.[17] Make Grief, Guilt, Sorrow and Regret take a hike! Clean your mind of those negative, pressing thoughts. Fill your mind with the positive thoughts of the Light. Press toward a goal, a new future, a better path.

- Take captive every vain imagination,[18] every thought planted by your avatar attackers. According to 2 Corinthians 10:5 NIV, "We demolish arguments and every pretension that sets itself up against the knowledge of God, and we take captive every thought to make it obedient to Christ." Jesus Christ is the Light. Victory can be had through the Light.

---

[16] Eph 6:12 NIV, "For our struggles is not against flesh and blood, but against the rulers, against the authorities, against the powers of this dark world and against the spiritual forces of evil in the heavenly realms."

[17] Phil 3:13-14 KJV, "forgetting those things which are behind, and reaching forth unto those things which are before, I press toward the mark of the high calling"

[18] 2 Cor 10:5 NIV, "We demolish arguments and every pretension that sets itself up against the knowledge of God, and we take captive every thought to make it obedient to Christ."

- This is not easy. You should seek Christian counseling if you need help.

#Loneliness

Has your grief, sorrow or loss left you feeling lonely? Is there emptiness or emotional lack in your life? There is healing to be found.
Where? Or how?

- You need to try to take your focus off of yourself and your feelings. Try to find true followers of the Light, to join you in this journey.
- Then begin to fill the void with something positive or productive. Take up a hobby or do volunteer work. Begin to move toward something that gives you joy. As you take your mind off of what you perceive as your needs, you will make room for productive thoughts to fill that void. Doing good things for other people is a nice place to start. I'm not trying to make you a Boy Scout, but small acts of kindness can help.

You should also know that your loneliness, emptiness and lack have already been provided for. Remember that song by Big Daddy Weave? You just need to take steps in the right direction. Get yourself into a better place because the song continues like this:

> Then You look at this prisoner and say
> to me son
> Stop fighting a fight that's already
> been won[19]

Did you know that your fight could already be over? It could have already been won and you did not know it. Josh Wilson puts it this way:

> But the debt's already paid
> And the bail's already made
> So why do I keep coming back again[20]

To answer that last line, you keep coming back again because your mind needs to be renewed. You need to learn how to live in the victory that

---

[19] Big Daddy Weave. "Redeemed."
[20] Wilson, Josh. "No More."

is meant to be yours. You need to learn to do the following:

- Take captive every vain imagination[21], every thought planted by your evil avatar attackers.
- You just have to get to that place and time where it is finished.

Does that sound ridiculous to you?

Here's the secret! To be in the right place and time, you have to be guided by the Light. And God is light.

---

[21] 2 Cor 10:5.

Treasure Hunt Clue Number 2

#The_Light

1 John 1:5-9 KJV tells us, "This then is the message which we have heard of him, and declare unto you, that God is light, and in him is no darkness at all. But if we walk in the light, as he is in the light, we have fellowship one with another, and the blood of Jesus Christ his Son cleanest us from all sin. If we confess our sins, he is faithful and just to forgive us our sins, and to cleanse us from all unrighteousness." The Father, God and His Son, Jesus Christ are the Light.

Even if you are already in the Light, don't stop reading. You may need this information in the future for a friend or family member.

Hi, I Was Little-Goody-Two-Shoes.

I grew up in church. I thought I knew the Lord as my Savior. I discovered later that I only knew 'about' God and Jesus. There is a big difference. I was such a goody-two-shoes that everyone thought I was fine, including me.

When I was eight, my mom and I had been attending a revival. It was now Saturday night and my parents were talking before church. I overheard my daddy say, "She's too young. She doesn't know what she's doing." Well I didn't know what they were talking about, but I knew that my daddy said I was too young, so that was that!

My dad was a very stern (scary) man back then. He thought he knew the Lord because he told me that he had joined the church when he was 16. He was a hard-working and honest man, but I never saw a whole lot of evidence of Jesus in his life.

That night was the only night that my dad accompanied us to the revival. The preacher started. He announced his sermon title, "Seven Ducks on the River Jordan." I remember thinking, 'Finally, one for kids.' So I listened intently. Though it wasn't exactly what I thought it was going to be,

I felt a 'pull' inside me. I knew that God wanted me to go forward and give my life to Him, *but* daddy was sitting right behind me and I already knew what he thought. So I clung to the pew, afraid to move.

Afterwards, I told my mom. She said not to worry because tomorrow was Sunday and I could go then. Sunday came. Sunday School came and went, then came Big Church. The altar call was given, but God was not drawing me. The only thing I felt was my mom's fingers in my back urging me forward. I had already told some friends that I was going to 'get saved,' so I was stuck.

I walked forward with mom at my back. I'm sure she had already told the pastor that I was coming, and he must have thought that she had already prayed with me at home because all he did was put his hand on my head and pray for me. (But that could have been what kept me in church for the next eleven years.)

Want to know what was going through my mind while our pastor was praying for me? Later when the Lord did again call me, he gave me a flash of memory of that moment. I was thinking, 'I hope he's not messing up my hair.' 'I hope my slip is not showing.'

Oh, my! Little-Goody-Two-Shoes, just got a shock. Eleven years later, I realized that I had never prayed and asked Jesus into my heart! Up until that point, I had only known about Jesus, I never knew Him personally. Well, I got that fixed, pronto!

So how does it work? Asking Jesus into your heart.

John 3:16 KJV is very clear. "For God so loved the world, that he gave his only begotten Son, that whosoever believeth in him should not perish, but have everlasting life."

Sounds easy, right? Just believe.

Well, brain alert! 'To believe,' does not mean to think it's true. According to *Strong's Exhaustive Concordance*, 'to believe' means "to entrust ones spiritual well-being" to Him.[22] In other words, you are so sure that Jesus is the Christ that you cannot be persuaded otherwise, *and* you entrust your life now and after death to His care.

The Bible says, "to enter in at the strait gate, because the way to destruction has a wide gate, but

---

[22] "Believe." Strong, James. 1970. *Strong's Exhaustive Concordance of the Bible*. Abingdon Press.

few find the way to life."[23] But if you drop on down a few verses in Matthew 7:21-23 NIV, Jesus says:

> Not every one who says unto me, 'Lord, Lord,' will enter the kingdom of heaven, but only the one who does the will of my Father who is in heaven. Many will say to me on that day, 'Lord, Lord, did we not prophesy in your name and in your name drive out demons and in your name perform many miracles?' Then will I tell them plainly, 'I never knew you. Away from me, you evildoers!'

That's a shocker!

Here's another example, in John chapter 3. It is the story of Nicodemus who was a Jewish leader and teacher. He told Jesus that he knew that He (Jesus) was a teacher who was "come from God" and that no man could do the "miracles" that He did, "except God be with him," John 3:1-2 KJV.

Jesus told him, "Verily, verily, I say unto thee, Except a man be born again, he cannot see the

---

[23] Mt 7:13-14.

kingdom of heaven." So even though Nicodemus knew the Hebrew scriptures and believed (thought) that Jesus was sent from God, *something* was missing.

Which brings up the question, what does it mean to be 'born again'? According to *Strong's Concordance*, it means to be "regenerated."[24] Nicodemus was still confused, so Jesus got a little more basic. "Except a man be born of water and of the Spirit, he cannot enter the kingdom of God. That which is born of the flesh is flesh; and that which is born of the Spirit is spirit," (KJV). So to begin with, we are flesh. That's fairly simple.

In John 14:6 KJV, Jesus says, "I am the way and the truth and the life. No one comes to the Father except through me." Nicodemus was on the right track. He believed that Jesus was from the Father, and he's hoping to find his way to the Father, and that way is through Jesus. For the second part—born of the spirit, John 6:44 KJV says, "No man can come to me (Jesus), except the Father which has sent me draw him." (Emphasis mine.)

Woo, a little complicated!

---

[24] "Born again." Strong.

Not really! It is the Spirit of God which draws you to be curious because God is "not willing that any should perish, but that all should come to repentance," 2 Peter 3:9 KJV.

Now the next question is how are you 'born of the Spirit'?

1. You must believe in God, and God must draw you to Jesus to be born again. You must believe that Jesus is God's Son,[25] born of a virgin,[26] was crucified on the cross,[27] died[28] and rose from the dead on the third day.[29] Wow, that is a lot, isn't it? But it is all necessary to deeply believe.

How can anyone do that? Well you pretty much can't unless God, through His Spirit, draws you and shows you the truth. If you can't quite buy

---

[25] Mk 1:11 NIV, "And a voice came from heaven: 'You are my Son, whom I love; with you I am well pleased.'"

[26] Is 7:14 NIV, "The virgin will conceive and give birth to a son,"

[27] Mk 15:15 NIV, "He had Jesus flogged, and handed him over to be crucified."

[28] Mt 27:50 NIV, "And when Jesus had cried out again in a loud voice, he gave up his spirit."

[29] Mt 28:56 NIV, "The angel said to the women, 'Do not be afraid, for I know that you are looking for Jesus, who was crucified. He is not here; he has risen, just as he said. Come and see the place where he lay.'"

into all of this (yet), pray and ask God to show you the truth.

But if you are at the point where you do believe that God is the Father, Jesus is the Son and Jesus met all of the above criteria, then...

2. Have you realized that you are a sinner? "all have sinned, and come short of the glory of God," Romans 3:23 NIV.

3. And that "the wages of sin is death, but the gift of God is eternal life in Christ Jesus our Lord," Romans 6:23 NIV. Look at that last part. The gift of "eternal life in Christ Jesus our Lord." Do you believe deeply enough that you are willing to trust Jesus as your Lord?

4. Then "If we confess our sins, he is faithful and just and will forgive us our sins and purify us from all unrighteousness," 1 John 1:9 NIV.

5. Now after you confess your sins, "If you declare with your mouth, 'Jesus is Lord,' and believe in your heart that God raised him from the dead, you will be saved," Romans 10:9 NIV.

6. Why can't you believe with just your head? Because there is the possibility that you

could be swayed by another person's argument if you only had head knowledge. But if you 'believe in your heart' that Jesus is Lord, then you have had an experience. When you have had an experience, *you-know-that-you-know*, and you cannot be swayed.

7. "Therefore if any man be in Christ, he is a new creature: old things are passed away; behold, all things are become new," 2 Corinthians 5:17 KJV. After you earnestly believe these scriptures and pray to ask Jesus to be your Lord, you become new! Old things are gone. Old sins are wiped away, and you have been redeemed. Redeemed means that you were purchased (paid for) at the cost of the blood of Jesus.

8. Without Christ's death and blood shed on the cross, we could not be redeemed. "But now in Christ Jesus you who once were far away have been brought near by the blood of Christ," Ephesians 2:13 NIV.

If you would like to receive the gift of God which is eternal life through Jesus Christ, if you would like to ask Jesus into your heart, talk to God from your heart and ask Him to save you. Here is a sample prayer, sometimes called a Prayer of Salvation or the Sinner's Prayer.

Dear heavenly Father,

I believe that you are the one true God and that you sent your Son Jesus to die on the cross in my place, for my sins. I believe that Jesus died and rose again from the grave by the power of your Holy Spirit.

I know that I am a sinner. I confess my sins to you. Father, I repent of all of my sins and ask you to forgive me and cleanse me from all unrighteousness. By faith, I ask Jesus to come into my heart, save me and change me. Make me into a new creation. Jesus, I ask you to be Lord of my life.

Amen!

This prayer is not a formula and it doesn't have to be word for word, but you do have to mean the content from your heart. At this point, you can join Big Daddy Weave singing:

"I'm not who I used to be,"[30]

---

[30] Big Daddy Weave. "Redeemed."

because you are now redeemed.

I suggest that you Google the words of this song, "Redeemed" and get the whole story. Better yet, purchase the above song and all the songs that I mention. I get no commission from this. I don't even know these people, but you need to get these songs deep into your spirit and soul. There are many excellent contemporary Christian singers and songs today. Begin to listen to Christian music that is in a style that blesses you. It will feed your spirit and nourish your soul.

Treasure Hunt Clue Number 3

#Your_Soul

At the end of the previous section, I mentioned that you need to get the words to Big Daddy Weave's song deep into your soul.

So what does it mean to get something into your soul?

According to *Strong's Exhaustive Concordance*, your soul (in the New Testament Greek) means:

1. Your heart—where your feelings and life come from.
2. Your mind—where rational and moral thoughts come from.
3. Your soul can also be the source of your fleshly desires because of the pull that your thoughts and your feelings have on you and

your actions.[31] That is an excellent reason to get your soul saturated with God's Word and with songs that will lift you above the old places where your heart, mind and feelings use to take you. You are now out of darkness and into the Light.

Begin to fill your soul with scripture by reading or listening to God's Word. If you don't have a Holy Bible, you need to get one. If you have trouble reading and understanding the Bible, look for a modern translation. Some are better than others. Many people today prefer something other than the King James Version, though I personally enjoy the language. One preferred translation is the NIV, New International Version. If that is still too difficult, ask a clerk at a Christian bookstore for a good teen or youth Bible. Start where you need to start, but get started.

'But where do I begin once I have a Bible?' The book of John in the New Testament is a good place to begin. Read slowly and thoughtfully. The Bible is not a novel. It is the book of life. Even after reading the Bible for many years, I can still be

---

[31] "Soul." Strong.

astounded by something new that pops out at me when I need it.

Remember the dream that I wrote about previously? That was a real dream. After I had that dream, the Lord began to bring songs to my attention. I could possibly have heard them before, but the meanings didn't register until after the dream.

A song by Josh Wilson and Ben Glover, "That Was Then, This Is Now," hit me like a ton of bricks after the dream. Here are some of the lyrics:

> We use to hide from the Light
> We made friends with the night[32]

Boom! Right up side my head! That was in my dream. God gets our attention in many different ways. Right now, with me, He is moving in music and lyrics. True, there have always been songs and hymns with powerful words, but at this point in time, in my personal opinion, we have a torrent of

---

[32] Wilson, Josh. "That Was Then, This Is Now." By Josh Wilson and Ben Glover. *That Was Then, This Is Now*. Sparrow Records. 2015. CD.

powerful songs and music pouring from Christian radio stations and churches.

Josh and Ben go on to say:

> And we figured that we were just too
> far gone
> But we were wrong[33]

Someone reading this can relate to those words. Maybe not everyone, but some people have believed that they were too far-gone. Well, you are wrong. God's grace is bountiful. He's merciful and He loves you and wants you to come to Him.

Did you pray the Prayer of Salvation? It's not too late, if He's calling you. I have had people ask me about what some call "the unpardonable sin." Without a long explanation, let me say that I believe, that if you are being called or drawn by the Holy Spirit, then you have not committed the unpardonable sin. God is not a tormentor. He is the redeemer. Don't you want your sins washed away? You can be free. You can be Redeemed. You can flip back to that prayer now.

---

[33] Wilson, Josh. "That Was Then, This Is Now."

Treasure Hunt Clue Number 4

#This_Is_New

You can't get much better preaching than those lyrics to describe your old life and your new life.

Speaking of preaching, if that word turns you off, find a pastor who is more of an expository preacher. That's a fancy way of saying, they explain or teach. You may prefer a pastor who breaks things apart and explains their meaning.

Also look for a church that welcomes new converts. Sometimes babies are messy. They are well worth keeping and training, but it takes people who love babies to help them grow. For instance, I heard a story of a new convert who went to a church for the first time and the pastor welcomed him from the pulpit and asked if he would like to say anything. He stood and in the midst of his 'thank you,' a curse word popped out. Yep, right there in front of God, granny and everybody.

He didn't know any better. Not knowing the difference and doing it defiantly are very different. Sometimes people have to learn a new language or at least how to temper their old one to fit into a new life. There is sometimes a gap between salvation and purification where a learning curve is involved.

Some churches are better at dealing with those kinds of issues than others. Though it could possibly have been granny who would have taken that new convert under her wing to help him navigate new waters.

If you are a new convert, don't get blown away by having to clean up your language, or by having to pull your pants up a little higher, or by having to wear your belt a little tighter to block from view some of the old parts of you, while Jesus is revealing the new creature inside.

Ladies, you may need to show less cleavage and understand that Jesus loves the inside of you, not just the assets that you may have used in the past. Dress for respect, not for attention, but that doesn't mean wearing turtleneck sweaters. Just show less of you and more of God. While all of that will not save you, your outside needs to begin to reflect your new creature inside.

In the meantime, you need to move on to learning more about spiritual warfare. Many long-time Christians are in this same boat. Let's see what God has prepared for us.

Treasure Hunt Clue Number 5

#Warfare

For those who have known Jesus as Savior and Lord for a while, I have a question for you. Do you sometimes or constantly feel that you are under attack? Well, you probably are. That's not very reassuring I know, but until you learn how to battle the forces portrayed by pirate avatars from my dream, you will suffer one assault after another as the enemy tries to wear you down and destroy you.

Remember that song by Big Daddy Weave? It mentioned things in your past that can haunt you. 'Haunted' can mean 'mental anguish.'[34] That speaks of torment of the mind. Your heart and mind have been left devoid of the good that they

---

[34] "Haunted." Apple MacBook, *New Oxford American Dictionary*.

need and feelings of anguish have moved into your soul (your heart, your mind, your will and your emotions). Your soul is tormented by the remnants of the previous attacks that you have suffered at the hands of the enemy. But there can be relief, with the help of the Light.

Let's look at your main attacker. Do you know the church names for the head honcho of the avatars in my dream? He is called: Lucifer, Satan, the accuser of the brethren,[35] the thief and the Devil.

Do you know what his job is?

Here's the answer: "The thief comes only to steal and kill and destroy," John 10:10 NIV.

Check it out:

- His primary work includes stealing from you.

Has he stolen your peace, your joy or your resources? Are you constantly worried, afraid, depressed or financially short? Has he stolen your talent because you are too afraid to use it? Your talent may be the pearls and jewels in my dream that were hidden away from the Light.

---

[35] Rv 12:10 KJV, "for the accuser of the brethren."

- The devil's work also includes trying to kill you.

Did you know that he will try to kill you spiritually? To him that is as good as bodily death. Perhaps even better because of the pitiful witness it gives to others. A lost person may think, "If Christians can't prevail and overcome in everyday life, then why should I even try?"

- Has he attempted to destroy you?

Has he crushed you down so far that you are using drugs and alcohol to medicate away the pain? Have you been abused so much that you sell your body to survive? Are you so far down that you can't even try to dig your way out anymore? Do you use any measures, even evil ones, to get ahead?

Has he destroyed your family? It doesn't matter if you blew it, or your ex blew it or that it somehow got squandered. What is of concern is that the head honcho avatar won. You have become bitter, your 'ex' has become bitter and if there are kids, there is probably bickering, anger, maybe even some neglect, but definitely emotional harm is happening.

Want to know what that does to a child? Just look at today's statistics of drug and alcohol use, violence, crime and the school dropout rate among our youth. It shouldn't take long to decide who actually caused all of that. It wasn't the pawns in the game, it was the one controlling the game. Learn to break his control!

So what do you do? The second part of John 10:10 tells you why Jesus came. "I have come that they may have life, and have it to the full," (NIV).

That sounds good! Now who would you rather follow? Who do you trust? If you trust Jesus, do you know how He wants you to fight?

Treasure Hunt Clue Number 6

#Weapons_of_Warfare

Here is the key to this Treasure Hunt Clue. 2 Corinthians 10:4 NIV, "The weapons we fight with are not the weapons of the world. On the contrary, they have divine power to demolish strongholds."

If you prayed a prayer of salvation, then you know Jesus in a personal way. That makes you are a new creature. Then how can you use your old, fleshly weapons? You need new, fresh weapons of spiritual warfare.

Psalm 20:7 KJV says, "Some trust in chariots, and some in horses: but we will remember the name of the Lord our God."

That word 'remember' means to be mindful of or to recognize.[36] In other words, you need to

---

[36] "Remember." Strong.

begin to recognize and understand that even the names of God and Jesus have power.

So your first lesson in spiritual warfare is to realize that when you called on God and Jesus to save you, that was an invitation to become part of their family. I'm sorry if you were never able to call on your natural family for help, but now you have a Father and a brother, Jesus, whom you can count on.

In times of crisis, call out to Jesus or cry out to your heavenly Father. You can quote scripture to them or just tell them what you need and then expect help! Yes, expect in faith! Below is an amazing true story told by Mrs. Susanne Cox, the wife of Pastor Ron Cox, formerly Senior Pastor of Kingwood Assembly of God, in Alabama. I met Susanne before she was married. She had been a missionary in India. This story took place in India.

I (Susanne) had to travel alone one night, and when I got off of the train I hailed a taxi. I told the driver where I needed to go, but soon realized he was not taking me there.

The taxi driver stopped the cab and was joined by four other men who offered him money to buy me for sex trafficking. I was not strong enough to fight five men, so I began to yell, 'I Plead the Blood of Jesus.' Louder and louder! And I screamed out Psalm 91:11, 'Father, you've given your angels charge over me to keep me in all of my ways!'

Those four men were slammed backward against a wall, looking terrified into the heavens!

The taxi driver jumped into the cab and fled the scene, delivering me to the proper address with me praying in the Spirit the whole way!

I never saw the angels myself, but I'm sure that whatever those potential abductors saw that night was enough to thwart their evil plan! God is faithful to His Word!

Keep in mind that Susanne did not willingly put herself into that situation, so don't decide to wander down a dark alley and expect God to rescue you if you get into trouble. He might, but Jesus Himself said in Matthew 4:7 that we are not to tempt the Lord our God. We are not to put him to the test foolishly. He is our rescuer, but wants us to trust Him, not test Him.

"Behold, God is my salvation; I will trust, and not be afraid: for the Lord Jehovah is my strength and my song; he also is become my salvation," Isaiah 12:2 KJV.

From this verse we see that with salvation comes strength. Also with salvation comes the power of the Holy Spirit of God. Zechariah 4:6b KJV says, "Not by might, nor by power, but by my spirit, saith the Lord of host." That is why Isaiah could say that he would "not be afraid."

You need to get to know who God the Father, Jesus the Son and the Holy Spirit are, and their roles in your life. You are different now. You need to learn to live differently.

Treasure Hunt Clue Number 7

#Your_Armor

Did you know that God has prepared an armor for you? Ephesians 6:13 NIV says, "Therefore put on the full armor of God, so that when the day of evil comes, you may be able to stand your ground, and after you have done everything, to stand."

Here are the parts of your armor described in Ephesians 6:14-18 NIV:

"Stand firm then," (6:14)
- "with the <u>belt</u> of truth buckled around your waist," (6:14),
- "with the <u>breastplate</u> of righteousness in place," (6:14),
- "and with <u>feet fitted</u> with the readiness that comes from the gospel of peace," (6:15).

- "In addition to all this, take up the <u>shield</u> of faith, with which you can extinguish all the flaming arrows of the evil one," (6:16).
- "Take the <u>helmet</u> of salvation (6:17),
- and the <u>sword</u> of the Spirit, which is the word of God," (6:17).
- "And <u>pray</u> in the Spirit on all occasions with all kinds of prayers and requests. With this in mind, be alert and always keep on praying for all the Lord's people," (6:18).

The armor in Ephesians 6, includes many of the topics we have already touched on, but look at 6:13 again. "Therefore put on the full armor of God, **so that when** the day of evil comes, **you may be able to stand** your ground." (Emphasis mine.) It doesn't say that when the day of evil comes, you should put on your armor. It says, get your armor on, so that when the day of evil comes, you will be prepared to stand. There is a big difference.

Hopefully, you have prayed the sinner's prayer and have on your <u>helmet</u> of salvation. The first thing you must do is to be saved and be in Christ; then protect your mind by filling it with the word of God, which is the <u>sword</u> of the Spirit. Did you know that many attacks which come your way can be canceled out or extinguished if you know what God has said about the situation? It is difficult to try and find the right scripture after an attack has begun. You need to get the word into your spirit beforehand, then your <u>sword</u> can be swiftly drawn at the first sign of trouble.

For instance, if the devil tries to tell you that you are not righteous, you can fight back with the <u>sword</u>. Philippians 3:9 NIV is great. "Not having a righteousness of my own that comes from the law, but that which is through faith in Christ—the righteousness that comes from God on the basis of faith." See how necessary and vital knowing scripture is?

We see that our righteousness is not through our own works. We are to put on the <u>breastplate</u> of righteousness which you now know is provided for us by the blood of Christ. The <u>breastplate</u> is to protect your heart from the attacks of the enemy. Remember the sections of this book regarding 'adoption' and the 'loss of a relationship'? If you get God's word deeply into your heart and spirit, you will understand God's love for you and learn how to be healed by Him of all your scars. You have been adopted! You are now in a new family.[37]

Back to the <u>sword</u> for a moment. Did you know that God's Word is food to your spirit and soul? Jesus "answered and said, 'It is written, Man shall not live by bread alone, but by every word that proceedeth out of the mouth of God,'" Matthew 4:4 KJV.

This is what the Bible is: it is God's Word, written by men, under the direction of God's Holy Spirit. "All scripture is given by inspiration of God, and is profitable for doctrine, for reproof, for correction, for instruction in righteousness," 2 Timothy 3:16 NIV.

In other words, the Bible is G-mail, but not 'Google mail,' it is God's mail, written to us. The scriptures are for your training. They are your <u>sword</u>, your weapon of offense against your enemy, the Devil. In fact if you look at the list again, the <u>sword</u> is the only weapon of offense. The rest are weapons of defense.

With all of this new understanding, your <u>feet</u> are becoming <u>fitted</u> with the readiness that comes

---

[37] Rom 8:15 NIV, "The Spirit you received does not make you slaves, so that you live in fear again; rather, the Spirit you received brought about your adoption to sonship."

from the gospel of peace. With this readiness, you should be willing and eager to share your faith in Christ with others. Don't worry about knowing much doctrine at this point, just share what Christ has done in your life. People can call you crazy, but they can't change what you have experienced.

As you read, study and learn more about the Father, the Son and the Holy Spirit, you are wrapping the <u>belt</u> of truth around yourself. Truth, not as the world sees it, but as your new <u>sword</u> describes it. Keep studying and don't get caught up in the parts you can't understand yet, press on and dig deeper. It will become clearer over time. Then stand firm in what you know to be true.

We have looked at your helmet, breastplate, belt, sword and foot covering. The other two pieces of armor on the list need a little deeper inspection. Let's look at the <u>shield</u> of faith and <u>prayer</u>.

Treasure Hunt Clue Number 8

#Your_Shield

Remember this statement about the armor of God? "take up the shield of faith, with which you can extinguish all the flaming arrows of the evil one," Ephesians 6:16 NIV.

Faith is a defensive weapon that you use as a <u>shield</u> around yourself. Your sword and shield go together and here is the reason. Faith comes by hearing, and hearing by the word of God.[38] Or put it this way, your <u>shield</u> is formed by hearing the word of God, which is your sword. You need to build a <u>shield</u> of faith around yourself by reading, hearing and learning scripture. That is one reason

---

[38] Rom 10:17 NIV, "Consequently, faith comes from hearing the message, and the message is heard through the word about Christ."

that I have included scriptures within this text or printed it in the footnotes of this book.

Do you want to see what great faith looks like? Look at Matthew 8:5-10 NIV:

> When Jesus had entered Capernaum, a centurion came to him, asking for help.
>
> "Lord," he said, "my servant lies at home paralyzed, suffering terribly."
>
> Jesus said to him, "Shall I come and heal him?" The centurion replied, "Lord, I do not deserve to have you come under my roof. But just say the word, and my servant will be healed. For I myself am a man under authority, with soldiers under me. I tell this one, 'Go,' and he goes; and that one, 'Come,' and he comes. I say to my servant, 'Do this,' and he does it."
>
> When Jesus heard this, he was amazed and said to those following him, "Truly I tell you, I have not found anyone in Israel with such great faith."

That gentleman had it going on. He knew some very important principles.

- He believed that Jesus could heal his servant.
- The Centurion knew about warfare and authority.
- And he practiced this: "For we live by faith, not by sight," 2 Corinthians 5:7 KJV. And this, "Now faith is the substance of things hoped for, the evidence of things not seen," Hebrews 11:1 KJV.
- 'Hoped for' does not mean wished for, it means "to expect, be confident of, or to trust."[39]

That is faith in a nut shell. You believe in Jesus, you believe in Jesus' power, you know His authority, and you live by faith in that knowledge. So faith is belief, assurance and faithful devotion. You rely on Him. You are constant in your profession of your faith in Him. You are devoted to Him and you trust (have confidence) in Him.[40]

---

[39] "Hope." Strong.
[40] "Trust." Ibid.

But what happens if He doesn't seem to answer your prayers? Lauren Daigle sings a powerful song whose words include:

> When you don't move the mountains
> I needed you to move
> When you don't part the waters
> I wish I could walk through
> When you don't give the answers
> As I cry out to you
> ...
> I will trust in you[41]

That is faith! That is trust! Even when you don't see what you wanted to see, you have confidence that God is still in control and working on your behalf.

Proverbs 3:5-6 NIV says, "Trust in the Lord with all of your heart (which is your mind, will and emotions); and lean not on your own understanding (mental capacity to figure things out). Acknowledge Him in all that you do and He will direct your path." (Emphasis mine.)

---

[41] Daigle, Lauren. "Trust In You." By Lauren Daigle, Paul Mabury and Michael Farren. *How Can It Be*. Century City Music. 2015. CD.

God doesn't always do things the way *we* think He should, but because "we walk by faith, not by sight," 2 Corinthians 5:7 KJV, we often have to surrender our wants and yield to His greater wishes, as we continue to have faith in Him and His ways. "That your faith should not stand in the wisdom of men, but in the power of God," 1 Corinthians 2:5 KJV.

Consider this, "'The righteous will live by faith,'" Galatians 3:11 NIV. But do you think, 'Oops, I'm not righteous'?

Oh yes you are, if you are in Christ Jesus. Remember Philippians 3:9 NIV, that we looked at earlier, "not having a righteousness of my own that comes from the law, but that which is through faith in Christ—the righteousness that comes from God on the basis of faith."

Jesus has got you covered. You are covered with His blood. The Father no longer sees you, He sees the blood of His Son and declares you righteous. Isn't that a relief? Now look how devoted the Father and the Son are to you.

Romans 8:38-39 KJV, "For I am persuaded, that neither death, nor life, nor angels, nor principalities, nor powers, nor things present, nor things to come, nor height, nor depth, nor any other creature, shall be able to separate us from the love of God, which is in Christ Jesus our Lord." And Ephesians 2:8 KJV, "For by Grace are ye saved through faith; and that not of yourselves: it is the gift of God." Also Philippians 3:9-10 KJV, "And be found in him, not having mine own righteousness, which is through the faith of Christ, the righteousness which is of God by faith: That I may know him, and the power of his resurrection."

The role of the Holy Spirit is found in Romans 8:11 NIV, "And if the Spirit of him who raised Jesus from the dead is living in you, he who raised Christ from the dead will also give life to your mortal bodies because of his Spirit who lives in you."

The power of His resurrection includes Isaiah 54:17 NIV, "'No weapon forged against you will prevail, and you will refute every tongue that accuses you. This is the heritage of the servants of the LORD, and this is their vindication from me,' declares the LORD."

What powerful promises those are! In the above verses, do you see the distinct roles of the Father, the Son and the Holy Spirit? Look what comes with being a servant of the Lord Jesus Christ.

"A servant? I thought I just came out of bondage and slavery." Well, you did. You came out of bondage to sin! But the term 'servant,' in this instance, means a 'bond servant.' One who chooses to serve a Master.[42] God is not forcing anyone to serve Him. He offers salvation as a free gift to those who are willing to receive it.

Previously, you served the master of this world. The one who brought sin and death. Now you serve the One who gives life. And yes, if you were serious about asking Jesus to be Lord of your life, you were volunteering to live under His rule. Keep in mind that His rule is always for the best interest of His Kingdom, but also for your best interest. Even when it doesn't feel like it.

That brings up another good point. Face it here and now, you are no longer to live by feelings. You are to live by faith in God the Father, Jesus the Son and by the power of the Holy Spirit, but you may still have some old feelings. Your feelings are one of the things you must learn to submit to Him. Feelings are in the same vein as your old habits and old language. They are part of what I was talking about earlier where you may need to

---

[42] "Servant." Strong.

learn a new language and learn to conquer old habits, but now you will have the aid of the Holy Spirit to do it.

As you get to know the Father, the Son and the Holy Spirit better, you will see that knowing them produces feelings far superior to the feelings you've had before. If you give it a try, you will even learn to feel their glory and get caught up in their presence.

Toby Mac has a great song called, "Feel It." It goes like this:

> Oh, I feel it in my heart
> I feel it in my soul
> That's how I know
> You take our brokenness and make
> us beautiful
> …
> Everybody talkin' like they need some
> proof
> But what more do I need than to feel
> You[43]

---

[43] Toby Mac. "Feel It" (feat. Mr. TalkBox). By Toby McKeehan, David Arthur Garcia and Cary Barlowe. *This Is Not A Test.* Universal Music. 2015. CD.

Above, when I said 'if you give it a try,' that includes getting into a Bible believing, Bible teaching church; learning about the Father, Son and Holy Spirit; recognizing their power and inserting yourself into praise and worship by participating.

Get your mind off of your troubles and onto the ones who set you free. Feeling the presence of God is more awesome than what the world provides. Get a taste and see. This will also build your shield of faith. You must know the ones you trust in order to truly trust them.

As we push onward toward prayer, let me share this with you. This will be an explanation of what prayer is, but whole books have been written on the subject. The knowledge I will attempt to provide is a good place to start. You must understand what prayer is, then you can begin to exercise your prayer muscles. Your prayer life can grow from there.

Treasure Hunt Clue Number 9

#Prayer

What is prayer?

Prayer is one of your best lines of defense against the enemy. 1 Thessalonians 5:17 KJV tells us to, "Pray without ceasing." In this verse, to pray simply means to earnestly ask God without stopping.[44]

Jesus gives some instruction on prayer in Matthew 6:5-8 NIV.

> And when you pray, do not be
> like the hypocrites, for they love
> to pray standing in the synagogues
> and on the street corners to be

---

[44] "Pray." Strong.

> seen by others. Truly I tell you, they
> have received their reward in full.

Verse five says that you don't have to stand up in a crowd or on a street corner to be heard by God. In fact if you pray to get attention from humans, then that will be your reward. But you shouldn't confuse that with being asked to pray aloud in church. That is different.

> But when you pray, go into your
> room, close the door and pray to
> your Father, who is unseen. Then
> your Father, who sees what is done
> in secret, will reward you.

Verse six gives you instruction on praying in private. If you haven't seen the movie, "War Room,"[45] this would be a good time to purchase or rent it. There is an amazing amount of information in this movie and it is done in a very enjoyable way. You can learn a lot from "War Room."

Back to Matthew 6, verse seven:

---

[45] "War Room." Kendrick Brothers. TriStar. Sony Pictures. 2015. DVD.

> And when you pray, do not keep
> on babbling like pagans, for they
> think they will be heard because of
> their many words.

Your prayers don't have to be long and wordy, just genuine and humble. And check out verse eight.

> Do not be like them, for your
> Father knows what you need before
> you ask him.

What a relief! God already knows what you need, but He wants you to ask Him anyway. It's hard to go wrong when you ask God for something. The only way you can really miss it is: "When you ask, you do not receive, because you ask with wrong motives, that you may spend what you get on your pleasures," James 4:3 NIV. Hmmm, 'wrong motives.'

God is very concerned about our needs, our safety and our health, but He's not always crazy about our wants. Sometimes we receive things we want because they are beneficial to us, but if our 'wants' fall into the category of fulfilling our lusts, or wrong desires, then we don't need what we are requesting.

For instance, if you desire a husband or wife, ask God whether you need a husband or wife at this time. He may say, "no," because He wants you to rely on Him and a spouse would divert your attention from Him. If He says, "yes," you can begin to ask Him to bring you a spouse, then wait patiently. But you cannot ask for the pastor or the pastor's wife to be your mate. That is covetousness and lust. So within reason, ask God for what you need. Occasionally, you can even throw in a request for something that you want.

But look at this aspect of praying for yourself— have you ever considered asking God to restore your financial resources that the enemy has stolen? Remember John 10:10 KJV says that the Devil came to "steal and kill and destroy." Now that you are embarking on a new style of warfare, maybe you should ask God to restore your resources.

This is what He did for Jacob. "You, LORD, showed favor to your land; you restored the fortunes of Jacob. You forgave the iniquity of your people and covered all their sins," Psalm 85:1-2 NIV.

God may also desire to restore your lost resources, as long as you understand that a responsibility comes with them. You cannot squander them on wrong motives. So ask the Lord to forgive you if you wasted your resources on wrong motives, or if you wasted them due to a lack of wisdom. Ask Him to restore what the enemy has stolen. What do you have to lose? Ask! But as a rule of thumb, begin by asking for things which you know that He will approve.

For example, pray for the salvation of your family and friends. That is a request that you know He is interested in granting. Look at 2 Peter 3:9 KJV, "The Lord is...not willing that any should perish, but that all should come to repentance." But keep in mind that those individuals have a free will to accept or reject the Lord, just as you did. Sometimes it takes a while, like with my father. My father prayed and received the Lord as his Savior in his 70's. I prayed for him over a span of many years before he asked the Lord to save him, so don't give up!

I also knew someone who never lived for the Lord during his 60+ years, but on his death bed, he asked his grown children (who had been praying for him for years) what he needed to do to be saved. He prayed a prayer of repentance and yes, I believe God saved him. Look at Psalm 78:38-39 NIV, "Yet he was merciful; he forgave their iniquities and did not destroy them. Time after time he restrained his anger and did not stir up his full wrath. He remembered that they were but flesh, a passing breeze that does not return."

See! The Father and the Son know our frailties. Jesus, when He agreed to come to earth to die for us, "was in all points tempted like as we are, yet without sin," Hebrews 4:15 KJV. Jesus experienced our struggles first hand, but He did not sin. After His resurrection, Jesus ascended to heaven and He was seated at the right hand of the Father where He constantly talks to the Father on our behalf. Romans 8:34 KJV is proof, "Christ...who is even at the right hand of God, who" makes intercession for us.

He is even interceding for us to be able to forgive others. Mark 11:25 NIV explains that our power in prayer is linked with forgiveness. "And when you stand praying, if you hold anything against anyone, forgive them, so that your Father in heaven may forgive you your sins." We are to allow God to take care of the people who have hurt or offended us. He is our defender.

Picture someone who is in need, lying on the ground too weak to even speak, and you stand between that person and God to speak on his or her behalf. As you look up to God and explain the situation and ask for help or mercy from Him, you are interceding on behalf of that person. This is what Jesus continually does for you. This is what you are doing for the people that you ask God to save. That makes you an intercessor too.

Treasure Hunt Clue Number 10

#Supplications

As we have already seen, there is more than one word for prayer. 1 Timothy 2:1-2 KJV introduces us to 'supplications.' Timothy says, "first of all, supplications, prayers, intercessions, and giving thanks, be made of all men; for Kings, and for all that are in authority; that we may lead a quiet and peaceable life in all godliness and honesty."

We have already discussed prayer and intercession, but 'supplications' adds a new dimension to our understanding of prayer. According to *Strong's Concordance*, supplications are petitions.[46] So Timothy tells us that all men should make petitions to God regarding those in authority over them. That doesn't mean that

---

[46] "Supplications." Strong.

we have to like or agree with the authorities on every issue, or on any issue for that matter. But regardless of our feelings, we are to lift up to the Lord those in authority, and their decisions. We are to petition Him to intervene with His purposes and plans, so that we can lead quiet, peaceful lives "in all godliness and honesty."

Too often, people are quick to draft petitions, get them signed by those who agree, deliver them to their leaders and demand change. When actually we should be sending petitions to God in the form of supplications, asking that His will be done.

If Christians fail to lift up their leaders, it seems to imply that, decisions could possibly be made that would force us into a governmental system that would not allow Christians to lead godly, peaceful lives. Could it be, in our present culture, that Christians of the past and present, have dropped-the-ball in petitioning God for His intervention in our nation's affairs? Hmmm! Interesting thought, so what do we do?

God addresses this aspect of prayer in 2 Chronicles 7:14 NIV, "If my people, who are called by my name, will humble themselves and pray and seek my face and turn from their wicked ways, then I will hear from heaven, and I will forgive their sin and will heal their land." Therefore, we should pray for the leaders of our nation, our state, our county and at the local level. We are to pray for those in authority over us to make godly decisions, and that the Lord's will shall be done on earth as it is in heaven.

Treasure Hunt Clue Number 11

#The_Kingdom

"The Lord hath prepared his throne in the heavens; and his kingdom ruleth over all," Psalm 103:19 KJV.

I want you to consider a kingdom in heaven, with majestic gates leading into God's beautiful courtyard. God the Father is seated on His celestial throne and Jesus, our Savior, is seated at His right hand. Picture angels all around worshiping and praising them, not just for what they do, but for who they are.

Now I'm going to tell you that this kingdom is as real as anything you can see, taste, smell, hear or feel here on earth. God wants you to be aware of it. He wants you to come before Him by faith, into His presence, now, in this life. You can cry out to God anytime and anywhere, but if you want to learn more about the spiritual kingdom of God, look at Psalm 100:4 KJV, "Enter into his gates with thanksgiving, and into his courts with praise: be thankful unto him, and bless his name."

How do you "bless His name"? In this verse Psalm 100:4, the word 'bless' is 'barak' in the Hebrew, meaning "to kneel, as an act of adoration."[47] If this is all new to you, it may feel a little strange to behave in this manner, but give it a try. Like a small child kneeling beside his bed in the evening, you can talk to your Father. After all, it was with the simplicity of a child that you came into the kingdom of God. "Whosoever shall not receive the kingdom of God as a little child shall in no wise enter therein," Luke 18:17 KJV. Add to that Matthew 18:4 KJV, "Whosoever therefore shall humble himself as this little child, the same is the greatest in the kingdom of heaven."

Now I can picture a Big Biker Dude, dressed in his leathers, who has just been presented with this proposition. "Yeah, Dude, things are changin.'" I know that God is working in you. Go ahead and kneel before the King of kings, who has conquered your formerly stone cold heart. He loves you with

---

[47] "Bless." Strong.

the most tender love that you have ever and will ever experience.

I'll show you an example of what kneeling and praise can accomplish. Look at how one particular Biblical battle was fought and won. 2 Chronicles 20, tells an interesting story about a vast army that was coming against King Jehoshaphat and the people of Judah. In verse six (NIV), this is what Jehoshaphat prayed, "'LORD, the God of our ancestors, are you not the God who is in heaven? You rule over all the kingdoms of the nations. Power and might are in your hand, and no one can withstand you.'"

This is the reply that God gave through the prophet Jahaziel in verse seventeen, "'You will not have to fight this battle. Take up your positions; stand firm and see the deliverance the LORD will give you, Judah and Jerusalem. Do not be afraid; do not be discouraged. Go out to face them tomorrow, and the LORD will be with you.'"

Here is the King's response in verse eighteen; "Jehoshaphat bowed down with his face to the ground, and all the people of Judah and Jerusalem fell down in worship before the LORD." In other words, they blessed God. Then the priests began to sing and praise and the King encouraged the people of Judah to have faith. Look what happened, "As they began to sing and praise, the LORD set ambushes against the men of Ammon and Moab and Mount Seir who were invading Judah, and they were defeated." So kneeling before the Lord to bless Him and being involved in praise and worship are apparently powerful weapons of warfare.

What a mighty God we serve! And if the King of Judah could bow before Him in the face of a huge invasion, I think it follows that being on our knees or lying with our faces to the ground before Him, is a pretty safe place to be when we are in a battle and need His help.

No matter what you were before; biker, prostitute, Wall Street analyst, goody-two-shoes, or whatever—you are now under a new ruler. So how do you communicate with your new King? Answer—implement Psalm 100:4 KJV. "Enter into his gates with thanksgiving and into his courts with praise." Being thankful was also mentioned in 1 Timothy 2:1, "supplications, prayers, intercessions, and giving thanks, be made of all men." Remember that heavenly kingdom that we talked about? You are welcome to come through

His gates anytime. All you need to do is begin to thank Him.

Demonstrate to the Lord that you are thankful. Thank Him for your salvation. Thank Him that He wants to save your loved ones. Thank Him that He sent His only Son to die for your sins, so that you can have eternal life with Him. Thank Him for His Holy Spirit who will teach you. Thank Him that you are not the same old person that you use to be. Even if you are barely breathing, you can thank Him for that. You get the picture!

Spend some time doing this. Think about it. It's not just a ragged, old list. Be really thankful for what you present before Him. Then realize that you have passed through His gates and you are entering the courtyard before His beautiful palace.

Begin to praise Him. Praise God for who He is. He is the creator of the universe. He set the stars in place. He had a plan for all people, even though many rebelled against Him. Praise Him that He has a plan for your life. Praise Him for His Son. Praise Him for being merciful enough to send His Son to earth. Praise Him for His love, faithfulness, kindness and for His glory.

Praise Jesus for coming and dying in your place which shows His mercy and love. Praise Him that He paid a debt that He did not owe; because you owed a debt that you could not pay, and Jesus paid it all. Tell Him that you love Him, because like Toby Mac puts it:

"You wrecked me."[48]

Now that you are in His presences, reverently present your prayers, supplications and intercessions to Him.

This information should give you a place to start in prayer. If it all still seems a little fuzzy, simply talk to God. He loves you, He is listening, and He understands. Let Him know what is in your heart and mind and how much you appreciate all that He has done for you.

In *#LifeChange,* we have traveled from a dream about a dystopian world to the actual entrance to the Kingdom of God. That is quite a journey! One which I hope you have traveled too, not just read about, and hopefully you have gleaned some important spiritual facts, or at least seen them in a new light. Continue to study. Research the footnotes, don't just take my word for what I've

---

[48] Mac, Toby. "Feel It."

said. Read it for yourself. May God continue to bless you and *#LifeChange* you. May Jesus become more real to you than ever before and may the Holy Spirit become your guide.

~~The End~~
Just the Beginning!

Music Selections

Remember to look for music that will build you up and inspire you. You may need to clean up your play list to keep your mind and spirit encouraged.

In alphabetical order, these are the songs from which I have quoted:

Big Daddy Weave. "Redeemed." By Mike Weaver and Benji Cowart. *Love Come To Life.* fervent Records. CURB Records. 2012. CD.

Josh Wilson. "No More." By Josh Wilson, Benji Cowart and Jeff Pardo. *That Was Then, This Is Now.* Sparrow Records. 2015. CD.

Josh Wilson. "That Was Then, This Is Now." By Josh Wilson and Ben Glover. *That Was Then, This Is Now.* Sparrow Records. 2015. CD.

Lauren Daigle. "Trust In You." By Lauren Daigle, Paul Mabury and Michael Farren. *How Can It Be.* Century City Music. 2015. CD.

Toby Mac. "Feel It" (feat. Mr. TalkBox). By Toby McKeehan, David Arthur Garcia and Cary Barlowe. *This Is Not A Test*. Universal Music. 2015. CD.

Other Works Cited

Apple MacBook, *New Oxford American Dictionary*. http://www.apple.com/macbook/built-in-apps/. Model A1466. CA. 2013. Apple, Inc.

Strong, James. 1970. *Strong's Exhaustive Concordance of the Bible*. Abingdon Press.

King James Version of the Bible. <http://www.blueletterbible.org.

New International Version of the Holy Bible. <http://www.blueletterbible.org.

Acknowledgments

First, I would like to thank God for always being there and never giving up on me. I thank him for being a giver of dreams and for the dream that was the catalyst for this book. The first dream that I remember Him giving to me was a recurring dream, over a period of about two years, when I was six to eight years old. It came true in every detail and the warning possibly saved my life.

Also thank you Father for sending your Son to die me; a sacrifice that is hard to fathom. Thank you Jesus for your shed blood that saved me, and to the Holy Spirit who has patiently guided me, though often I was slow to follow.

I would also like to thank my family for their love and patience with me through the years. Including my brother, Brian, who saved my life from an exploding pressure cooker when he was about seven years old. My husband says that 'the pressure cooker story' gets a lot of mileage, but it is true and though it could have ended tragically, my brother and I have been able to share many laughs about it.

My special thanks to Mrs. Susanne Cox for giving permission to use her story. "You were a blessing when I first met you several years ago and you still are today!"

Thank you to the Christian artists who are producing such wonderful songs during these time in which we live. Thank you for the truth and encouragement in your work.

My recognition and thanks go to Pastor Charles Lenn, for being our pastor for almost 20 years, for your mentorship, for your pastoral support through several life crises, and for writing an endorsement for this book. You have truly been a blessing.

And for the many hours of reading and correcting my typos, as well as encouragement and support, thanks to my friends Michael and Kay Wojack, Carolyn Wilkes, Sandy Tilley, Pastor Charles Lenn, Pastor Chris Palmer and my husband Jim. May the Lord richly bless you all!

About the Author

Mrs. Whatley has been a Christian for over 45 years. Before that she had been a faithful church member, who 'thought' she was a Christian, until the Holy Spirit revealed to her that she had never asked Jesus into her heart, she had merely joined a church.

She and her husband were married in 1970 and have one son. He and his wife have blessed the Whatleys with four beautiful grandchildren.

Mrs. Whatley earned her Master of Arts degree in Christian Counseling and Education from Regent University, Virginia Beach, Virginia in 1985. She has also taken many additional Bible courses through Berean School of the Bible.

After their son—who had been home schooled 7th-12th grades—graduated from college, Mrs. Whatley wrote the book, *Will My Child Fit? An Answer to the Home Schooling Question: "What About Socialization?"* The book was published in 1996 and sold nationwide at Home School Curriculum Fairs.

Mrs. Whatley has taught at three Christian Schools and two Community Colleges. In addition, she has taught many Sunday School classes and Bible courses at their church. Her career also included being a Testing Technician for a Neuropsychologist for 10 years, during which time she had the privilege of leading a few elderly patients to the Lord.

She and her husband are currently retired and living in Tennessee with their two dogs, Bear and Millie.

Printed in the United States
By Bookmasters